Stürtz  REGIO

WEIMAR

D0474273

Text by
Bodo Baake

Photos by
Horst and Tina Herzig

WEIMAR

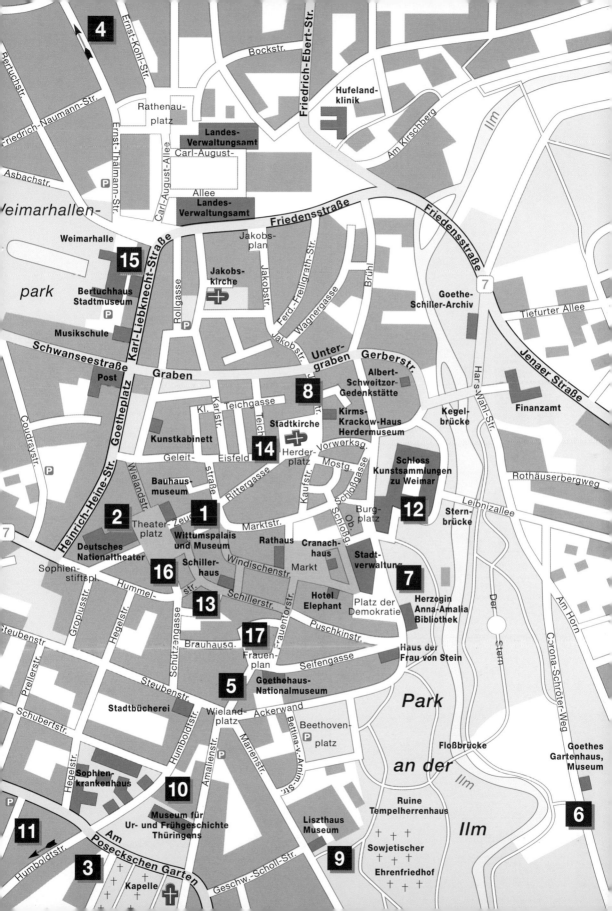

Stürtz REGIO

WEIMAR

Text by Bodo Baake
Photos by
Horst and Tina
Herzig

Front cover: Top: the Goethe and Schiller monument in front of the Deutsches Nationaltheater.

Bottom left: reading boy in front of the Neo-Classical Bertuchhaus, now the city museum.

Bottom centre: a big attraction on the Weimar calendar – the Zwiebelmarkt in October.

Bottom right: Goethehaus with the Goethe National Museum on Frauenplan.

Back cover: palace Belvedere with its fabulous gardens makes a wonderful day out.

Page 4/5: the statue of Goethe and Schiller on Theaterplatz, unveiled in 1857.

Page 8/9: travelling in style through Weimar – here, riding past the Zum weißen Schwan pub on Frauenplan.

The Authors:

Bodo Baake, born in 1941, is a freelance journalist and publicist working in Jena.

Horst and **Tina Herzig** are freelance photographers and photographic designers in Groß-Gerau. They have also had the titles "Odenwald and Bergstraße" and "Leipzig" published in the Stürtz REGIO series.

Credits

Photos:
Archiv für Kunst und Geschichte, Berlin:
vignette top left p. 20, all photos; all photos p. 21;
vignette top left, portrait of Johann Wolfgang von Goethe, portrait of Duke Carl August p. 26;
bottom p. 27; top right, bottom left p. 42; top left and right p. 43; all photos p. 57; top p. 67.
Stiftung Weimarer Klassik/museums:
bottom left p. 24: Goethehaus, Junozimmer with bust; main photo p. 30/31: Wittumspalais, Tafelrundenzimmer; top right p. 33: Anna-Amalia-Bibliothek, Rokokosaal, bottom left: Schillerhaus, study; all photos by Sigrid Geske.

Die Deutsche Bibliothek – CIP – Einheitsaufnahme
Weimar / Horst and Tina Herzig (Fotogr.),
Bodo Baake (Autor) –
Würzburg: Stürtz 1999
Deutsche Ausgabe u. d. T.: Weimar
ISBN 3-8003-1392-8 / Softcover

Editing: Elisabeth Glotzmann, Würzburg
Translation: Ruth Chitty, Schweppenhausen
Design: Förster Illustration & Grafik, Würzburg
Cartography: Theiss Heidolph, Eching am Ammersee
Travel map printed with the kind permission of the Erfurter Verkehrsbetriebe AG
Repro: Universitätsdruckerei H. Stürtz AG, Würzburg
Printed and produced by the Universitätsdruckerei H. Stürtz AG, Würzburg

ISBN 3-8003-1392-8 / Softcover

CONTENTS

THE HOME OF CLASSICISM

Christoph Martin Wieland – one of the great poets and humanists of the Weimar Classical period (below). Modest memorial for a great man – Johann Sebastian Bach at the Rotes Schloss (right).

You can begin your tour of the city anywhere you like in Weimar, for all roads lead to the *genio huius loci*, the spirit of Weimar. You can't miss it; it is omnipresent. Some of its tracks have been covered over or even obliterated; others are there for all to see. The clearest are those of what we today refer to as the Classical period, during which the little town became a fixed star on the horizon of academia, the most splendid City of Culture in Europe, which is the proud nomenclature Weimar is permitted to use throughout 1999.

"History sometimes pleases itself with jokes of dubious taste,"

Joseph Schumpeter once proclaimed. The chronicle of Weimar is full of such examples. Around 1800, at a time when in Germany national endeavours were laid low, the Thuringian city had cause for heady optimism. It owed its rise to a defeat suffered as far back as in 1547 by John Frederick the Magnanimous, the leader of the League of Schmalkalden, who at Mühlberg on the Elbe lost a battle, his electoral title and his lands of origin. Defeated, he fled to his beloved Duchy of Saxe-Weimar and transformed the sleepy town on the River Ilm into a royal capital.

The history of the Weimar phenomenon has since read as a tale of defeat which has lead to victory, of rise which has lead to fall, of arrivals which have brought with them departure. The Goethe poem "Welcome and Farewell" could have been written about Weimar.

The first newcomers of any renown were travellers en route to other destinations, and some even unwilling ones at that. In 1518 Martin Luther spent a night at the Franciscan monastery and preached in the Schloss, where in 1524 peasant leader Thomas Müntzer was interrogated. In 1552 Lucas Cranach the Elder came to Weimar as part of the royal entourage of John Frederick – and stayed. In 1708 Johann Sebastian Bach took up a post as court organist here and in 1772

poet Christoph Martin Wieland settled here as tutor to the prince.

His pupil Carl August invited Johann Wolfgang Goethe to the city in 1775. Goethe accepted, and a year later brought his mentor, Johann Gottfried Herder, to Weimar and in 1799 poet and professor of history Friedrich Schiller from Jena. They founded a republic of scholars, an alliance of power and the intellect, and with them Weimar entered a golden age.

Just as Weimar's artistic blossom was fading, Franz Liszt joined the talented throng. He revived the opera house, founded a music conservatoire (which now bears his name) and generally pumped new impetus into the city's cultural activities. Weimar sparkled once again. Following him, at the dawn of the 20th century, artists centred around Harry Graf Keßler, Henry van de Velde and Walter Gropius attempted to catapult the Classical period into the modern age – and failed.

Arrival and departure. Bach left, Wieland moved to Oßmannstedt, Liszt came and went, Goethe frequently wandered off to Italy, the Bauhaus was banished, and philosopher Friedrich Nietzsche, mentally deranged, faded away under the guardianship of his fateful sister. Was he perhaps a symbol? Weimar burned itself out – and dark clouds gathered on its smouldering horizon. The Weimar constitution became null and void; this vibrant stronghold of humanitarianism was overcast by the long shadows of barbarity in jackboots. Within view of the Goethehaus on Frauenplan, the Nazis erected a place of brutal cruelty and desperate suffering – Buchenwald Concentration Camp. They took the aesthetic wisdom "Noble is man, helpful and good…" and made a cynical "Each to his own" out of it, emblazoned in cold letters over the entrance to the camp.

A symphony of modern architecture. The new music school in Schloss Belvedere's historical park.

The entry Robert Schumann made in his diary in 1828 seems in retrospect quite ironic: "The Germans are violently attracted to Weimar; it is also unique in the whole of history." If this is the case, just where does a visitor, drawn with such force to this city of past glory and past terror, start treading in the footsteps of time?

Those who like to do things properly and efficiently will probably want to book a date with the town guide on the market square, where they will be presented with the usual municipal interiors:

the town hall, court apothecary, fountain and the oldest inn in town

(the Schwarzer Bär from 1540), plus a magnificent Renaissance house where Lucas Cranach the Elder spent the last year of his life (1552/53), had his studio and executed the wonderful altar triptych for the Stadtkirche. They will digest the main data on Weimar's history (first mention in documents: 975, town charter: 1254, royal capital: 1547) and then want to push on to the Platz der Demokratie with the statue of Carl August and to the 1,000-year-old

Right: he wanted to be portrayed as a pedestrian; his heirs, however, sat him on his high horse. Grand Duke Carl August on the Platz der Demokratie. The Bertuchhaus now accommodates Weimar's city history (below).

Residenz, where the Stiftung Weimarer Klassik and the Kunstsammlung zu Weimar now reside, along with all their marvellous Cranachs and Italian and Dutch masters. Their gaze will temporarily rest on the clumsy noblesse of the Hotel Elephant, for this is the anteroom of Weimar's living Valhalla, where all the great names in art, economics and politics travelling through the town have spent the night. And it may also remind them of "Lotte in Weimar", Thomas Mann's smug novel about the waiter-factotum Mager, who finds absolutely everything in Weimar "remarkable" and makes the apt comment: "Here in Weimar there is no such thing as a long way; our greatness is in the mind."

Visitors with a predilection for Classicism may, however, prefer to start their tour of Weimar at the Goethehaus on Frauenplan, the intellectual heart of the city. Here, Weimar is

Weimar in nuce, a village with court grandeur.

Here, Weimar is no longer a little town, but – to quote Madame de Staël – one giant palace where an equilibrium between spatial restriction and spiritual greatness was achieved by bidding the cosmos to enter the mind "through reading and study; one escaped the narrow confinement of one's surroundings through the broadness of thought."

This can all be experienced firsthand at the poet's house on Frauenplan. Its passages, narrow flights of stairs, hallways, rooms and salons seem to mirror the streets and squares of the city itself. Or is it the other way round? The asceticism of the interior, the Spartan bedrooms and studies, the candle light "by which in the evening the old man in his dressing gown, arms sprawled on an unmatching cushion, sat at the centre table and studied", were all in accord with the discipline of the mind – and the housekeeping budget of any good Weimar home. Yet the purse strings were looser when it came to the appreciation of art. Thus the whole of Weimar, like this residence with its busts and books, majolica and medallions, soon resembled a "Pantheon full of pictures and statues".

In an effort to reorder and reinterpret these treasures, the works Goethe wrote here and their effect on the world, the National Museum next to the Goethehaus underwent extensive

The world-famous Hotel Elephant on the market place is still a popular stop-off place for the greats of our time. The Anna Amalia restaurant pays culinary homage to the mother of Weimar's round table of intellectuals.

laying flowers at the foot of the Goethe and Schiller monument, at the feet of the heroes of German Classicism. This double statue, unveiled on 4 September 1857, is the town landmark and has come to illustrate world-wide the friendship the two writers enjoyed. Dresden sculptor Ernst Rietschel (1804–1861), a pupil of Christian Daniel Rauch, was one of the artists who worked on the monument.

He gave Schiller his idealistic, far-away gaze

and Goethe his realistic, down-to-earth view of the world. He managed to make Goethe, a few inches shorter than Schiller, seem as tall as his associate, and their reaching out for the laurel wreath looks as though both are saying: "After you, my dear sir!"

The costly bronze of the statues, donated by the king of Bavaria, came from Turkish canons fired during the naval Battle of Navarino (1827). The German poets stand proud – but why do they turn their back on Weimar's dramatic establishment, the Deutsches Nationaltheater, which under their management provided a glittering quarter century of theatrical culture? Is it perhaps because the building later took centre stage in the world of extremely dubious politics?

With that we'd have come to the more critical members of the guided

"Mother and child" – in 1895 sculptor Adolf Donndorf presented his home town with this beautiful fountain, which stands on the corner of Rittergasse and Windischenstraße.

Street musicians in the park in front of the poet's house on Frauenplan.

renovation to commemorate the 250th anniversary of Goethe's birth. Weimar is a permanent cultural building site; the Goethe Museum, Schiller Museum, Wittumspalais, Kirms-Krackow-Haus, Römisches Haus, Liszthaus, Nietzsche Villa and Weimarhalle all long to shine in a new light.

The guest who has come to honour the greats of literature may want to start his or her tour of Weimar by

tour. They would be best advised to begin exploring Weimar at what's known as the gau forum. This is one of the focal points of Weimar history. The construction of this Nazi centre of power began in 1937 with the destruction of idyllic Asbachtal valley and several streets in the old town. These were replaced by monumental barracks resembling a fortress which, together with the Halle des Volkes (never completed), lined a square conceived as a massive parade ground for Nazi propaganda with the predictable title of Adolf Hitler Platz. Initially, a bust of the Führer scrutinised the goings-on, later replaced by a generalissimo bust when the area was called Stalin-Platz, and later still by a Marx monument when the square was renamed a third time.

The inhumanity which laid the foundations of this architecture

so far has thwarted any attempts by the urban development authorities to rededicate the complex. Yet efforts towards change did awaken interest in the architectural gem of the Landesmuseum or state museum, almost smothered by the north wing of the gau forum. The most significant Neo-Renaissance building in Thuringia, erected by Czech architect Josef Zitek in 1863/68, was badly damaged during the Second World War and severely neglected by the GDR. It has now been lovingly

Left: cycling in Goethe's footsteps. The mon ami youth centre on Goethe-platz (below) was erected by Ferdinand Streichhan in 1858/60. The late Neo-Classical building was later a concert hall and ballroom and meeting place for the Goethe and Shakespeare Society.

Weimar idyll: soaking up some autumn sun on a stroll through the park on the River Ilm.

Explore Weimar from a horse and cart, such as here along Schillerstraße (below left), or at the Zwiebelmarkt, where you can buy wonderful bouquets of dried flowers (below right).

in 1930/31, a cross between New Objectivity and bold architectural decoration, in 1932 it was the scene of passionate nationalist eruptions at an event organised to commemorate the 100th anniversary of Goethe's death.

The hour of das deutsche Volk had come.

After the war the hall was a popular conference centre, whose users included the German Shakespeare Society. After extensive structural damage was later discovered, the building had to be torn down. A replacement conference and congress centre is planned. Greetings from the spirit of the age.

restored and is the first museum in eastern Germany devoted to modern art. From 1 January 1999 on the Maenz Collection will be on display. Herald the return of the modern age.

Almost within view of the Landesmuseum is the Weimarhalle, which seems to act as recent historical mediator between the Landesmuseum and the gau forum. Hastily erected

Regardless of where the tourist began his or her trip of the town, we will end it at Goethe's garden house. Simply everyone meets up at this icon of Weimar Classicism. "I have a sweet little garden on the Ilm outside the city gates … There is an old house there I will have repaired."

Thus enthused Goethe when he was given the property by the duke in 1776. He came here to write and to bathe, studied the phases of the moon, sketched out the beginning of "Wilhelm Meister", created "Tasso" and "Iphigenie", put candles in the window for Charlotte von Stein and lived here with his mistress, Christiane Vulpius. Here, the idea was also born to extend the "caterpillar wasteland" of the narrow Ilm Valley and turn it into a charming landscaped park.

In Weimar's year as City of Culture,

this enchanted place gives cause to seriously contemplate the phenomenon of original and copy, of aura and aureole. In the 1960s the rotten building materials of Goethe's garden house were gradually replaced and in recent years the interior has been stripped of its contents and decoration, posing the question as to what actually remains of Goethe's original garden house and whether imagination has long superseded reality. This is intensified by the age of the media with its capability for endless reproduction of all things cultural.

Untroubled by all this on the opposite bank of the Ilm is the stone snake cylinder (Schlangenstein), which bears the inscription *Genio huius loci*. Well, to be honest, it's actually a copy! The original stands in Goethe's garden. The good spirit

of Weimar – just where is it? "I can't find Weimar nowhere else…," said Jean Paul in the strange language of the 18th century with its double negative, duplicating his words to express an original sentiment... ■

Above: the temple of the muses in Schlosspark Tiefurt.

Genio huius loci. The stone snake in the Ilm park, fashioned by Martin Klauer for Carl August in 1787, calls upon the "good spirit of Weimar" (left).

The market place: the Cranachhaus and new north side of the square (right, far right). Neptune atop a fountain in front of the historic oriel of the court apothecary (below) and the Neo-Gothic façade of the town hall (bottom).

Until 1535 the market square was the place where medieval tournaments were held. Merchants and local women commandeered the area in the mid–16th century, where they have been doing friendly battle for custom ever since.

AMATEUR THEATRE AND POLITICAL STAGE

"Everyone is falling ill here. I have survived eight days of toothache; now Goethe is walking around yellow and pale and patching himself up. Herder has trouble with his back. Mieding, the theatre's carpenter, has even died…"

Goethe as Orest and Corona Schröter in the leading role at the Ettersburg amateur performance of "Iphigenie auf Tauris", given on 6 April 1779.

Carl August was in a sombre mood on 8 February 1782. Yet where the passing away of his theatrical joiner was only worthy of a mention, Goethe dedicated an entire poem to the death of Mieding in which he described the scenery of life at the theatre.

The theatre in Weimar was run by amateurs,

The Deutsches Nationaltheater, reconstructed in time for Weimar's year as City of Culture in 1999.

but was treated with serious professionalism. It all began when Duke Wilhelm Ernst had an opera room built in the Ilm wing of the palace in 1697. Until 1774, the year the palace burned down,

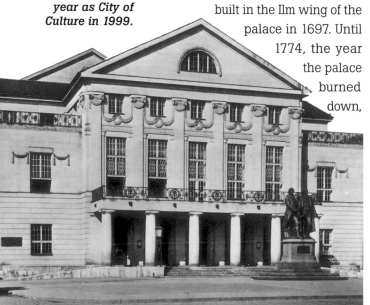

this was where the Seviersche Schauspieltruppe, the first professional troupe in Germany, acted. A year after the fire Goethe took over the management – and more than twenty roles. In 1791 he was made director of the palace theatre he and Schiller ran as co-producers until 1817. The list of performances included "Egmont", "Tasso", the Wallenstein trilogy, "Maria Stuart" and "William Tell", operas and operettas – and, of course, "Faust", on Goethe's 80th birthday in 1829.

Through the efforts of Franz Liszt, Weimar entered a "silver century of music", marked by a 500-year tradition of the court orchestra under Johann Nepomuk Hummel and confrontation with more modern trends in composition. In 1842 Liszt was

1926 the theatre found itself the venue of the second Nazi party conference; in 1944 prisoners from Buchenwald Concentration Camp were herded to the theatre workshops to make armaments. The building was destroyed in 1945.

Rebuilt as part of the nationalist efforts of the GDR, the Weimar theatre was the first to reopen after the war with a performance of Goethe's "Faust I" in 1948. A year later, in Goethe Year, Thomas Mann held his famous speech about the hope for a new humanitarianism. The Deutsches Nationaltheater, with its Classical inheritance, owes it a special debt of gratitude to this day. Yet one question from "Prologue at the Theatre" remains topical: "How shall we do it, so that everything is fresh and new…" ■

Left: scene from the "Iphigenie" performance painted by Wilhelm von Kaulbach, in which Duke Carl August also had a part as Pylades.

Members of the German National Assembly which proclaimed the Weimar Republic in 1919 and decided on its constitution.

made *Hofkapellmeister*; in 1849 he conducted Wagner's "Tannhäuser", performed works by Berlioz and Schumann and encouraged Dingelstedt to bring Shakespeare's kingly tragedies to the German stage.

In later years, politics trod the boards.

On 19 January 1919 the building was proclaimed Germany's national theatre, the Deutsches Nationaltheater, and it was here that, two days later, the National Assembly was called for 6 February. In August, the assembly approved the first democratic constitution in German history. The constitution of the Weimar Republic was, however, doomed to failure, drowned in wave upon wave of fanatic nationalism. As early as in

Gastronomy and the hotel business are writ large in Weimar. Pride of place is given to the renowned Hotel Elephant with its cosy guests' library (top left) and impressive staircase (top centre).

An original: the rustic Zum Zwiebel pub (left). Below: another cup, please! The coffee house atmosphere of places like the Café Am Frauentor is treasured by visitors and locals alike.

Right: the house of Frau von Stein is not far from the Goethe-haus, a symbol of the close relation-ship the poet had to his "friend of the heart", with whom he exchanged hundreds of letters.

Day-to-day life on Frauenplan (right). Below: the Junozimmer in the Goethehaus is one of Weimar's favourite postcard and photo motifs.

Hundreds of thousands of visitors from all corners of the globe come to the famous house on Frauenplan each year. Children and visitants like to relax on the lawn outside. One permanent resident is the Sunken Giant, a sculpture by Walter Sachs which the observer may like to interpret as an allusion to the faded grandeur of Weimar.

GOETHE IN WEIMAR

At the crack of dawn on 7 November 1775, a carriage trundled through Weimar's city gates. It was dark; the little town – with a mere 700 houses and 6,000 inhabitants – was still asleep. It slumbered through one of its "greatest moments", as Knebel, a very good friend of Goethe's, was later to call the memorable occasion.

In the horse-drawn coach sat Johann Wolfgang Goethe.

Goethe in formal dress and medals, after a painting by Heinrich Kolbe.

He had arrived from Frankfurt on his way to Italy, but had been waylaid by Carl August's mail coach driver. The young duke wanted to have the blossoming poet at his side, the man who had written "The Sorrows of Young Werther", the writer everyone was talking about. On hearing of the meeting, Wieland quipped: "Goethe won't ever leave here. Carl August can neither swim nor wade without him." His conjecture proved correct.

Carl August, Grand Duke of Saxe-Weimar-Eisenach, after a watercolour by Johann Heinrich Lips.

The new arrival, dressed in the dark blue tail coat, yellow waistcoat and leather breeches of his Werther, caused a sensation – in all senses of the word. Goethe was either treated with contempt or blindly adored. He counterbalanced this fickleness with happiness, friendship and the ambition of a genius who had the power to win hearts. On 11 June 1776 he entered the services of the City of Weimar as counsellor to a legation of the privy council. Soon afterwards he was made a minister, was administrator of the mine in Ilmenau, of Jena University and the Weimar library and was also responsible for state finances, military activities and the streets and roads in the 36 square miles of the duchy. "Chief Roadsweeper," mocked Herder – unfairly. Day-to-day life in Weimar actually improved under the statesmanlike care of Goethe. In 1816 Weimar was the first German state to pass a constitution; the eagerness to improve one's mind became a virtue, encouraging the flourishing of an artistic style which was to dominate almost the entire 19th century.

As opposed to Duchess Luise, who went to every effort to keep middle-class Doktor Goethe at a distance and refused to entertain him at either her games or dinner table, the duke's mother, Anna Amalia, bade him join the round table at her temple of the muses.

Here and at the Friday Society Goethe founded,

they sat and read the latest poems, discussed, drew, and acted out plays – Goethe and Herder, Wieland and Knebel, Einsiedel, Seckendorf and the hunchbacked court maid Louise von Göchhausen, who copied out the manuscript of "Urfaust".

It's hard to assess just how important this temple of the muses and Anna Amalia were to Classical Weimar; maybe they were responsible for its being there at all. Here was something which held Goethe in Weimar for a long period, something (and someone) which secured his existence and which contributed to the birth of his countless poems, his novels "Wilhelm Meister" and "The Elective Affinities", his dramas, "Tasso", "Iphigenie", "Egmont" and the legendary "Faust".

Yet life in Weimar wasn't all joy for Goethe. At an early stage he recognised the problems of a poet under the influence of power, "the utter crap of this transitory glory", as Johann Heinrich Merck called it. Sometimes he fled to his garden house, to Jena or Kochberg – or even Italy. The carriage in the coach house on Frauenplan was always waiting for him... ■

The legendary Weimar round table. Duchess Anna Amalia entertaining her guests – from the left, artist Heinrich Meyer, Henriette von Fritsch, Goethe, Friedrich Hildebrand von Einsiedel, Anna Amalia, Eliza Gore, Charles Gore, Emily Gore, court maid Louise von Göchhausen and Herder – after a watercolour by Georg Melchior Kraus.

A prominent corner of Weimar: the Café Am Frauentor where the Cooperative of Fine Artists once had its seat, now in the historic Cranachhaus on Markt (right and main photo). A few steps further on is the Stiftung Weimarer Klassik museum shop.

A halcyon array of little streets and alleyways, the old town is charming, with plenty of small shops, pubs and traditional arts and crafts to be discovered.

Wittumspalais (above, top), where Duchess Anna Amalia lived after she was widowed, is a place of great significance for Classical Weimar. The princess from Wolfenbüttel, mother to Carl August, ruled the small duchy on the Ilm with intelligence and prudence, securing its intellectual celebrity through her temple of the muses. Right: in this room the great scholars of Weimar met around Anna Amalia's fabled round table.

The Schillerhaus
on the esplanade
(centre and right),
which the poet
lived in until his
death on 9 May
1805, could once
be seen from
Goethe's house.

THE SPIRIT OF HUMANITARIANISM

Weimar is a "poet's biography raised to the status of city," with the Stiftung Weimarer Klassik as its custodian. The foundation safeguards the legacy of the bountiful era in which Goethe and Schiller demonstrated such great creativity. The brief span of the Weimar Classical period, the half a century between Goethe's arrival in Weimar in 1775 and his death in 1832, with its masterpieces of literature and the arts and its championing of the ideals of Classical humanitarianism, has produced some of the most brilliant achievements in world culture. It continues to influence us today.

This inherited emporium today numbers 30 national cultural monuments – museums, palaces, memorials, parks, archives and libraries. Perhaps the best known are the Goethehaus and Schillerhaus, the Goethe and Schiller Archives and Anna Amalia's library.

The archives and the library are the treasure-troves of Weimar.

The library bears the name of its founder, Anna Amalia, and started out as a ducal library compiled from books from Wittenberg in 1691. It has 2,000 medieval manuscripts, 900,000 valuable prints, Goethe's private collection of reading material, editions of his own work published in all languages of the world and secondary literature collated over 200 years. The library also has an

important collection of publications issued by the first German linguistic society, the Fruchtbringende Gesellschaft or "fruitful society" founded in 1617.

The Goethe and Schiller Archives are the oldest literary archives in Germany. The statistics are impressive: 6,000 archive files containing six million pages and

the works of over a hundred poets, among them Goethe and Schiller,

Achim and Bettina von Arnim, Georg Büchner, Eduard Mörike, Friedrich Hebbel, Fritz Reuter, Gustav Freytag, Franz Liszt and Friedrich Nietzsche.

Research, acquisition and publication are as much part of work at the Weimar foundation as collation and preservation. A comprehensive series of editions has been initiated whose long-term projects include national

Weimar's rich intellectual and cultural inheritance is magnificently illustrated in this splendid room from 1761 in the Anna-Amalia-Bibliothek.

Goethe and Schiller editions, an edition of secular works by Heine, diaries and collections of letters.

Two ambitious assignments carried out by the Stiftung's museum sector were the redesign of the Goethe National Museum and the redefining of the role of the Schiller Museum, built in the 1980s, as a forum for various presentations of the foundation's exhibits and guest expositions. The exhibition space at the Goethe Museum, extended to 900 square metres (ca. 9,690 square feet), is now devoted to a wider-reaching concept. It no longer focuses on the international literary figure of Goethe, but depicts the *genius loci* in the context of his day and age, with reference to the works of Schiller, Herder and Wieland. Would the literary quartet please take the stage … ∎

Friedrich Schiller fled the middle-class confines of his study time and again for "the land of ideals". A museum dedicated to the bard was erected behind his house, now used by the Stiftung Weimarer Klassik for various exhibitions.

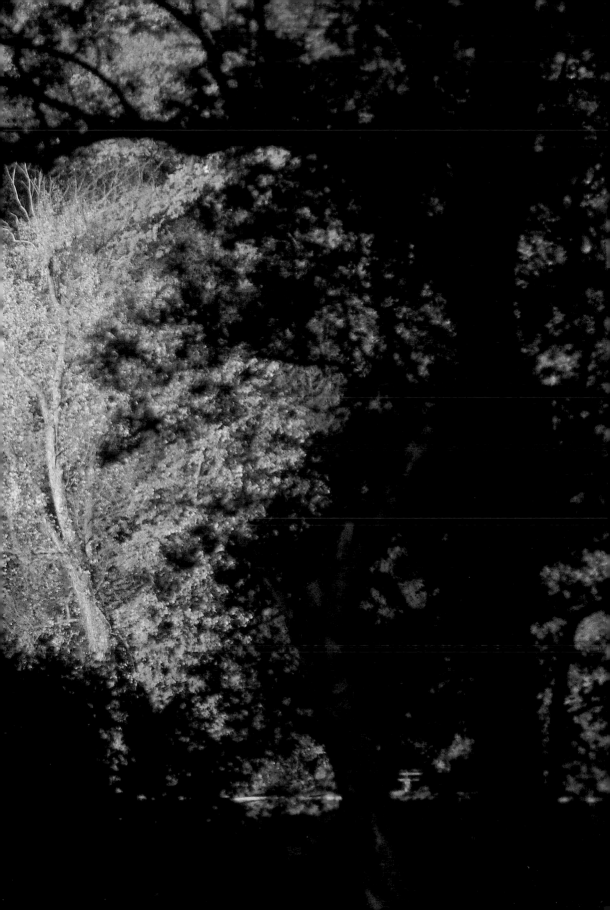

Previous double spread: the "icon of Classical Weimar", Goethe's garden house in the park on the River Ilm.

The Museum of Reading, opened in Schiller year 1859 on Goetheplatz (right), is a copy of the Temple of Wingless Victory on the Acropolis. Below: Karl August Musäus, a popular writer of the Enlightenment, lived in this picturesque corner house on Kegelplatz. His "German Folk Tales" are one of the most beautiful compendia of their kind and were a sensation in Weimar and beyond.

Weimar museums: when the museum behind the Schillerhaus was opened in 1988 it was – and was to remain – the only new literary museum built in the GDR.

The opening of the reconstructed Neues Landesmuseum (left) and of the exhibition on "The Rise and Fall of the Modern Age" on 1 January 1999 heralded the start to Weimar's year as European City of Culture. Bottom left: the Residenzschloss, where the Weimarer Kunstsammlungen and the Stiftung Weimarer Klassik are housed. Among the most precious items on display are Dutch paintings, art from the Romantic period and the Weimar School of Painters and interesting contemporary works from the GDR.

Poets are on everyone's lips in Weimar – Goethe brandy, marzipan Schiller medallions and wine from the Dornburg vineyards are firm favourites in the repertoire of (edible) souvenirs and devotional objects.

Left: silhouette of Goethe above the entrance to the café of the same name. The arrival of composer and virtuoso violinist Franz Liszt in Weimar – here the colourful garden of his house (main photo) – marked the beginning of a "silver century of music", hot on the heels of the "golden age" of Schiller and Goethe.

The Residenz Café opposite the palace Bastille (right) used to supply the palace guard with warm beer. It was later the court confectioner's and then frequented by the Weimar scene. They all came here – from historical painter Friedrich Marder-steig to the artists of the Bauhaus and Marlene Dietrich to the Kunstfest VIPs of today. The Goethe-Zimmer is a reminder that the poet himself once stayed here.

The palace (above, top left and main photo) seems almost too big for Weimar. The town was not unjustly mocked as being a giant "palace with a court". The complex started off as Burg Hornstein, a castle which in the Middle Ages was extended to become the Wilhelmsburg. After it burned down, it was rebuilt by Berlin architect Heinrich Gentz at the direction of Goethe, with work completed in 1803. The staircase, Weißer Saal and Falken-galerie are some of the most splendid examples of interior design of the early Neo-Classical period in Germany.

ENTER THE MODERN AGE

The history of the Bauhaus in Weimar is often described as one of expulsion. It is the story of Weimar, of the failed attempt to catapult Classicism into the modern age.

A group of students and teachers from the Weimar Bauhaus. Among them are Oskar Schlemmer, Josef Albers and Gunta Stölzl.

Invitation to a party at a villa in Oberweimar on the Ilm to celebrate five years of the Bauhaus (below).

The tale begins with the free school of drawing Goethe was responsible for. This gradually developed into a fully-fledged art school, where Arnold Böcklin, Franz Lenbach and Reinhold Begas laid the foundations for the Weimar School of Painters, where Theodor Hagen, Christian Rohlfs and Paul Tübbecke worked and which under Fritz Mackensen was elevated to the rank of art college in 1910.

This was enough to irritate the conservative minds of Weimar.

The town started practising rebellion against the artistic avant-garde, taking Harry Graf Keßler as its scapegoat. Keßler was co-founder of the Allgemeiner Deutscher Künstlerbund, an association of German artists, and founded the bibliophile Cranach Press in Weimar. In 1903 he was made director of the Großherzogliches Museum für Kunst und Kunstgewerbe, an arts and crafts museum patronised by the grand duke. When in 1906 Keßler had the audacity to exhibit nudes by Rodin, however, the grand duke was not amused. Snubbed by his employer, Keßler indignantly handed in his notice.

With the appointment of Henry van de Velde in 1902, the art school became a stronghold of a new style in architecture and arts and crafts – Jugendstil or Art Nouveau. Van de Velde promptly demonstrated the new striving for form on the buildings constructed for the college and the art school between 1904 and 1911. As an artist jack of all trades he was architect, painter, designer and craftsman rolled into one, searching for a formula for the new architecture in a whole row of buildings around

Humboltstraße, in his own house (Haus unter den hohen Pappeln) on Belvederer Allee and in the interior design of the Nietzsche Villa. His creativity in Germany was brought to an abrupt end in 1915, when the jingoism of the First World War forced the Belgian to flee the country.

In 1919 the Weimar Republic braved a new departure. The National Assembly was still in session when Walter Gropius merged the fine arts college and arts and crafts school to form the Staatliches Bauhaus in Weimar. The assembly turned the

Bauhaus into an umbrella concept embracing the disciplines of architecture, fine art, practical design and functionality. Artists such as Lyonel Feininger, Gerhard Marcks, Paul Klee, Georg Muche, Wassily Kandinsky and Laszlo Moholy-Nagy helped implement an idea which was to greatly change the art of the 20th century. In 1923 the Bauhaus presented itself to the general public in an exhibition encompassing among other masterpieces Georg Muche's Haus am Horn, now a monument to modern architecture.

In 1925 Gropius was forced to cease working in Weimar. Only a few years were granted him in Dessau before the Bauhaus was finally disbanded in Berlin. During the GDR period, the Bauhaus was eyed with extreme suspicion. The institution affiliated to it tentatively termed itself a college of architecture and building. The fall of the Berlin Wall finally gave the renamed Bauhaus University enough self-confidence to openly commit itself to its fantastic inheritance. ■

Above: 3D sketch of Walter Gropius's director's study. Left: poster advertising the grand Bauhaus exhibition of 1923 by Bayer/Maltan at the entrance to the main building.

The Kunstsammlungen zu Weimar have a permanent exhibition on the Bauhaus in what used to be the palace theatre store.

Weimar's appearance is characterised by handsome, respectable town houses (main photo). Much of what had been left to gradual decay is being restored to its former elegance.

Gables, decorative façades and moulded doorways adorn many of the houses and buildings here. From left to right: the Deutschritterhaus, detail of the façade of the Cranachhaus, coat of arms on a gable of the Gelbes Schloss, Renaissance portal of the Cranachhaus (left), entrance to the Rotes Schloss (below).

The fame of Weimar's Zwiebelmarkt public festival has spread far beyond the Rennsteig ridge and Thuringian Forest. For over 300 years the onion farmers of Heldrungen have tramped over Ettersberg Hill to Weimar, laden with their bulbous wares. The artistically woven strings of vegetable have become something of a tradition in themselves, celebrated with copious quantities of Bratwurst and beer.

The Zwiebelmarkt isn't all onions. There are also stands selling traditional Thuringian crafts. Potters, glassblowers, tanners and gardeners peddle their wares, with splashes of colour provided by imaginative arrangements of strawflowers.

THE CULT OF THE ONION

On even days there's steak, on odd days sausage and on Sundays dumplings to go with it… Joking aside, the local cuisine isn't as uninventive as it's often made out to be. Thuringia is a garden of herbs and a land of cake. Travellers passing through may easily mistake the clouds rising from the valleys for fog; what they can see is the smoke from hundreds of barbecues, the incense of Thuringia, wafting reverently towards the heavens.

Her Majesty the Queen of the Onion Market with the insignia of her special power.

The kitchen tables in this part of Germany don't bend under the weight of culinary delicacies; they are laden with plain, home cooking.

Recipes for black pudding and liver sausage are closely-guarded family secrets;

imagination runs riot when it comes to baking cakes for the village fete (150 different sorts is the norm!) and the things done with the simple

Above all, Thuringia is the land of the sausage.

onion here will make your mouth (and your eyes) water. Onion bread, onion flan and onion soup stave the hunger pangs, hot onion tea is a tonic for sore throats, and the obligatory grilled steak is considered inedible without fried onions. This is where matters of nutrition have become matters of religion.

In Weimar the onion almost enjoys cult status. The Heldrung countryside lives off its onion fields, a pub near the Stadtkirche calls itself Zum Zwiebel ("the onion") and the Zwiebelmarkt is a ceremonial celebration of the aromatic bulb. Weimar's onion market takes place every year on the second weekend in October and belongs to the rustic category of public festival. When the annual homage to the onion takes hold of the city, splashing the centre of Weimar in bright red and onion-

coloured hues, currency is measured in strings.

These artistically woven plaits of onions have been sold at the fair since 1653 or before, the year documents make first mention of a livestock and onion market in Weimar. The festival has been held regularly since then, albeit with minor interruptions in

Onions galore – the market spills across nearly the entire centre of town, from the theatre to the Stadtkirche and from the palace to under the windows of the Goethehaus.

times of war or other emergencies. If you want to visit the colourful stalls and attractions set out between Frauenplan, the market place and the theatre, then the best time to do so is in the early morning, when the onions still seem to smell of the fields, the flans are fresh from the oven and a cool beer warms the heart and stomach. You're in good company, for Goethe was also enthused by the piquant stands arranged in front of his house. He watched the goings-on from his windows and even decorated his room with strings of onions. Carl Friedrich Zelter reported: "The shining onions are strung like pearls... For 14 Pfennigs, Goethe had enough bought to last him the year and patriotically hung them in his window, which caused something of a sensation." It took a poet to make the onion, long a staple in Thuringian cooking, socially acceptable. ■

Zwiebelkuchen
(Onion Flan)

Ingredients: 300 g (11 oz) flour, 100 g (4 oz) margarine, 1 3/8 l (2¼ pt) milk, 25 g (1 oz) yeast, salt, 80 g (3 oz) semolina, 1 kg (2.2 lbs) onions, 100 ml (6 tbsp) oil, 1 egg, 10 g (½ oz) caraway seeds

Work the flour, margarine, ¼ l milk, the yeast and a pinch of salt to a dough. Leave to rise for 1 hour. Cook the semolina, 1 l milk and ½ tsp of salt until it has a porridge consistency and leave to cool. Fry the grated onions in the oil with a pinch of salt until transparent. Roll out the dough, briefly allowing to rise. Spread the semolina out onto it and then the onions. Whisk the egg with ⅛ l milk and pour over the onions. Sprinkle the caraway seed on top. Bake at 200–220°C (400–425°F/gas mark 6–7) for ca. 45 minutes. Onion flan tastes best hot.

Guten Appetit!

Previous double spread: the orangery at Schloss Belvedere summer residence.

The environs of Weimar promise plenty of fine days out: here, the ducal summer residence of Belvedere (top left, centre right and below), the park at Schloss Tiefurt (top right and main photo) and the Wieland estate in Oßmannstedt (top centre). Cherubs and masks, carefully clipped hedges and ancient trees tell us the story of life at court.

When Duke Carl August came to power in 1775 he founded a small court at Tiefurt. This was where Goethe, Wieland, Herder and Bertuch later acted in plays, read from their manuscripts and generally transformed their enchanting surroundings into a forum for the scholarly of Weimar.

The royal crypt with the mortal remains of the ducal family and poets Goethe and Schiller (below), Charlotte von Stein's tombstone at the Historischer Friedhof (right), the gravestone of Goethe's wife, Christiane Vulpius, in St Jacob's cemetery (centre) and the Franz Liszt monument in the Ilm park (far right).

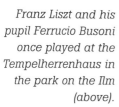

Franz Liszt and his pupil Ferrucio Busoni once played at the Tempelherrenhaus in the park on the Ilm (above).

The Goethe family grave. Here lies Goethe's daughter-in-law Ottilie with her children Alma, Walther and Wolfgang and their servant of many years, Wilhelmine Bachstein. The tombstones in the old cemetery bear the names of many famous people.

A PLACE OF SUFFERING

"Path of time Ettersburg–Buchenwald" is the title of a project planned for Weimar's year as City of Culture in 1999. The path will cut right across the park surrounding Schloss Ettersburg, Duchess Anna Amalia's temple of the muses, making the grounds of Buchenwald Concentration Camp visible from the palace gardens and forging a link between two opposite poles in Weimar's mental topography.

The gatehouse clock still shows the hour when the prisoners of the Nazi concentration camp on Ettersberg were freed.

It was on Ettersberg Hill that Goethe wrote his "Iphigenie" and even acted the part of Orest at an amateur performance here. Goethe's song of humanitarianism resounded only a few feet away from a place which was to become the scene of mass savagery. When in 1937 the Nazis erected their concentration camp here, sensitive Goethe fans protested at the use of the word Ettersberg as appellation.

The place of death was thus given the name Buchenwald.

238,000 people from 32 nations were held prisoner here until 1945. 56,000 didn't survive. Among them were Communist Ernst Thälmann and clergyman Paul Schneider. Those who suffered included famous poets, such as Ernst Wiechert, the young Jura Soyfer, librettist Löhner-Benda, famous for Franz Léhar's "Land of Smiles" and who later wrote the "Buchenwald Song",

Fred Wander, Jean Améry, Bruno Apitz, Elie Wiesel and Jorge Semprún, who dedicated his oratorio "Pale Mother, Gentle Sister" to the victims of the two major totalitarian systems of the 20th century. The

wald began processing its past, when it began laying out a field of crosses in memory of the dead and planning the camp exhibition, a note was discovered sealed in a bottle. Builders working on the memorial

Fritz Cremer's bronze Buchenwald group in front of the clock tower (left) documents the moment of liberation. Survivors in one of the dreadful barracks (above).

work was premiered at the Weimarer Kunstfest in 1995.

The horrors of Buchenwald didn't end with the liberation of the camp in 1945. In August of the same year, a new use was found for the barracks as the Soviet Special Camp No. 2.

designed by Fritz Cremer in 1958 had bricked a message into the spiral staircase of the clock tower. "We hope that in the future the dead of the Russian special camp shall be remembered alongside the dead of the concentration camp." ■

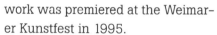

Around 28,000 prisoners were interned here until 1950,

many of them Nazi functionaries and Nazi sympathisers, but also innocent citizens and opponents of the Communist regime. Over 7,000 of them met their death.

Existence of the camp was hushed up for many years. Yet when Buchen-

11 April 1945: American soldiers in front of the main gates of Buchenwald Concentration Camp.

Gravestone bearing a likeness of Lucas Cranach the Elder at St Jacob's cemetery (top). Monument to Johann Gottfried Herder in front of "his" church (above).

Previous double spread: Russian chapel in the Historischer Friedhof.

Stadtkirche St. Peter und Paul. The rich artistic interior of the city church where Herder preached has a famous altar triptych by Cranach. The painter portrayed himself in it, next to the reformer Martin Luther and also the ducal couple with their three sons. The church also saw the first stirrings of rebellious GDR burghers during the months preceding the collapse of Eastern Europe.

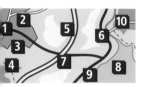

WEIMAR AT A GLANCE

1 The Bauhaus

The **Staatliches Bauhaus** was founded in 1919 under **Walter Gropius** and became the domain of many important artists. Hostility forced the Bauhaus to move to Dessau in 1925. After the Second World War, the Hochschule für Architektur und Bauwesen was established in Weimar, now the **Bauhaus University**. A **permanent exhibition at the Kunsthalle** on Theaterplatz honours the work of the Bauhaus artists. *(Bauhaus-Hochschule, Geschwister-Scholl-Straße 8, Bauhaus-Museum, Kunsthalle am Theaterplatz. Open: Tues. – Sun. 10 a.m. – 6 p.m.)*

Time signal: sculpture in front of the main Bauhaus building, designed by Henry van de Velde.

2 Deutsches Nationaltheater

Built in 1779 and **directed by Goethe 1791 – 1817**. In 1907 the theatre building, which had already burned down in 1825, had to be rebuilt. In 1919 it was named the Deutsches National-theater and served as a venue for the National Assembly. Destroyed in the Second World War, it was rebuilt with money from sponsors by 1948. *(Theaterplatz 2. For short-term ticket reservations, ring +49-(0) 36 43/75 53 34)*

Front view of the Bauhaus-Universität at Geschwister-Scholl-Platz.

3 Fürstengruft

The royal crypt was built by C. W. Coudray in 1825/26 as a **Classical mausoleum** in the old cemetery. 26 sarcophagi containing the mortal remains of members of the grand duke's family had been transferred here by 1824. **Carl August** was buried here in 1828. In 1827 and 1832 **the simple oak coffins of Schiller and Goethe** were laid to rest here. *(Am Poseckschen Garten/Historischer Friedhof. Open: 15 Mar. – 25 Oct. 9 a.m. –1 p.m. and 2 – 6 p.m., 26 Oct. – 14 Mar. 10 a.m. –1 p.m. and 2 – 4 p.m.)*

4 Buchenwald Concentration Camp

In 1937 the Nazis erected a **concentration camp** on Ettersberg Hill, where 56,000 prisoners were brutally murdered, among them **Communist Party leader Ernst Thälmann**. Post-1945, part of the camp was turned into the **Soviet Special Camp No. 2**. Buchenwald is a memorial to the victims of two dictatorships.

5 Goethehaus and National Museum

In 1782 **Johann Wolfgang Goethe** moved into the house dominating

Frauenplan and lived there for almost 50 years (minus brief intervals in Italy). Walther von Goethe, his last descendant, bequeathed the building and its entire inventory to the City of Weimar, who opened it to the public in 1886 as a **memorial**. The Goethe National Museum had been set up here a year previously. *(Goethehaus: Frauenplan 1. Open: 15 Mar. – 25 Oct. Tues.–Sun. 9 a.m. – 6 p.m., 26 Oct. –14 Mar. 10 a.m. – 4 p.m.; Goethe National Museum: Frauenplan 1. Open: 15 Mar. – 25 Oct. Tues. – Sun. 9 a.m. – 6 p.m., 26 Oct. –14 Mar. 10 a.m. – 4 p.m. Please ring +49-(0) 36 43/54 51 02 to book.)*

6 Goethe's Garden House
Goethe moved here in 1776. The house was permanently lived in until 1782. Parts of **"Iphigenie"**, **"Egmont"**, **"Wilhelm Meister"** and the poem "To the Moon" were written here. *(In the park on the River Ilm. Open: 15 Mar. – 25 Oct. 10 a.m. – 6 p.m., 26 Oct. –14 Mar. 10 a.m. – 4 p.m. Closed Tues.)*

7 Herzogin-Anna-Amalia-Bibliothek
Widowed Duchess Anna Amalia had the summer residence refurbished as a library from 1761 –1766. Goethe took over the management in 1797. Today the library has **almost 100,000 books**, among them a **"Faust" collection** numbering 13,000 and a **Shakespeare collection** of 10,500 volumes. *(Platz der Demokratie 1. Tel.: +49-(0) 36 43/54 52 00. Rokokosaal open May – Oct. Mon. – Sat. 11 a.m. – 12.30 p.m. Closed Nov. – Mar.)*

8 Kirms-Krackow-Haus
The **Renaissance edifice** built in around 1520 was baroquefied at the beginning of the 18th century. In 1917 the city of Weimar turned the house with its beautiful interior and courtyard into a **museum of bourgeois home decor** and a **museum of literature**, the latter of which pays homage to the works of Herder. *(Jakobstraße 10)*

9 Liszthaus
When **Franz Liszt** returned to Weimar in 1868, Grand Duke Carl Alexander put the house of the court gardener at his disposal. The **pianist and composer** lived and worked as music tutor here until his death in 1886. The ground floor has been turned into a small museum. *(Marienstraße 17. Tel.: +49-(0) 36 43/54 53 88. Open: 15 Mar. – 25 Oct. 9 a.m. –1 p.m. and 2 – 6 p.m., 26 Oct. –14 Mar. 10 a.m. –1 p.m. and 2 – 4 p.m. Closed Mon.)*

10 Museum für Ur- und Frühgeschichte Thüringens
The Thuringian museum of pre- and early history at the **Posecksches Haus** grew out of the items collected by the doctor Bruno Schwabe (1834 –1918). The museum has **prehistoric finds** unearthed near Weimar, including parts of 420,000-year-old skeletons and objects used by **Palaeolithic man in Ehringsdorf**. *(Amalienstraße 6. Tel.: +49-(0) 36 43/ 33 24. Open: Mon. – Fri. 9 a.m. – 5 p.m. and Sat. and Sun. 10 a.m. –1 p.m. and 2 – 5 p.m.)*

The youth club used to be called Walter Ulbricht, but was known locally as The Gay Friend. In ironic deference to its old sobriquet it's now known as mon ami.

1 10
The numbers 1 –10 refer to positions marked on the map on pages 2 – 3

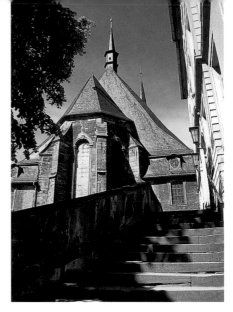

11 Nietzsche Archiv

Philosopher **Friedrich Nietzsche**, mentally ill, moved into the **Villa Silberblick** in 1897 in the care of his sister, who had Henry van de Velde refurbish their home in 1903. Around 1933, Elisabeth Förster-Nietzsche initiated the fatal **Nietzsche cult**. *(Humboldtstraße 36. Open: 15 Mar. – 25 Oct. 1 – 6 p.m., 26 Oct. –14 Mar. 1 – 4 p.m. Closed Mon.)*

12 Residenzschloss

The residential palace was originally a 10th-century moated castle which burned down in 1424. John Frederick the Magnanimous took up residence here in 1551. After fires in 1618 and 1774 Goethe supervised the construction of the complex still here today, whose interior houses masterpieces of the Classical period.

The palace is home to the **Kunstsammlungen zu Weimar**, an art gallery which consists of over 2,000 paintings, 10,000 drawings, 40,000 graphics, sculptures, coins and medals. The south wing accommodates the **Stiftung Weimarer Klassik**, a foundation responsible for Weimar's literary museums, memorials and archives. *(Burgplatz 4. Tel.: +49-(0) 36 43/54 60. Open: Tues. – Sun. 10 a.m. – 6 p.m.)*

Peaceful view of the St. Peter und Paul church.

Youthful visitors in front of Schiller's house, still seen as a poet of the young.

13 Schillerhaus and Museum

Schiller moved into the **house on the esplanade** with his wife Charlotte in 1802 and lived there with two sons and two daughters until his death in 1805. In 1847 the City of Weimar had a **museum** opened here in memory of the great writer. The new museum building behind the house was opened in 1988. *(Schillerstraße 12. Open: 15 Mar. – 25 Oct. 9 a.m.–6 p.m., 26 Oct. –14 Mar. 10 a.m. – 4 p.m. Closed Tues.)*

14 Stadtkirche St. Peter und Paul

In 1776 **Johann Gottfried Herder** joined the city church as its superintendent, holding his ecclesiastical office for 27 years. He was buried here in 1803. The interior of the building, which dates back to 1299, is particularly notable for the **altar triptych painted by Lucas Cranach the Elder** (completed by his son). Valuable tombstones show that the church was the burial place of the Ernestine dynasty. **Cranach's tombstone** is of cultural and historical importance. *(Herderplatz)*

15 Stadtmuseum

The building was erected by Weimar's **all-rounder**, writer, publisher and manufacturer **Friedrich Justin Bertuch**, between 1780 and 1803 as a place of business and residence. A museum devoted to the history of the city and its surroundings was set up here in 1955. *(Bertuchhaus, Karl-Liebknecht-Straße 5. Open: Tues. – Sun. 10 a.m. – 5 p.m.)*

Events

■ Each year in June/July, the **Weimarer Kunstfest** stages six weeks of theatre, ballet, concerts and readings.

■ The **Internationales Musikseminar**, organised by the Franz Liszt conservatoire in Weimar, embellishes the programme of musical events with concerts performed by students and visiting professors.

■ March/April is the time of year for the **Weimarer Bachtage**, part of the Bach festival in Thuringia.

■ The traditional **Zwiebelmarkt** is on the second weekend in October.

16 Wittumspalais and Wieland Museum

The palace was built on the site of the **old Franciscan monastery** in 1767 and acquired by Duchess Anna Amalia in 1774, who lived here in her widowhood until she died. The **round table of the great minds of Weimar** met here. A Wieland Museum was opened in the east wing in 1963. *(Theaterplatz 1. Tel.: +49-(0) 36 43/54 53 77. Open: 15 Mar. – 25 Oct. 9 a.m. – 6 p.m., 26 Oct. – 14 Mar. 10 a.m. – 4 p.m. Closed Mon.)*

17 Zum weißen Schwan

Built around 1500, the Zum weißen Schwan pub is one of the oldest pubs in Europe and is one of **Weimar's historic localities**. The sophisticated selection of food and drink is due to the number of famous guests who have wined and dined here, among them Goethe, who was full of praise for the Schwan's beer and wine. *(Am Frauenplan)*

Culinary encounters of the contrasting kind: the folksy Zwiebelmarkt (left) and the dignitaries' Zum weißen Schwan restaurant (right).

Further information

is available from the Tourist Information Office, Markt 10, D-99421 Weimar. Tel.: +49-(0) 36 43/2 40 00, fax: -6 12 40. Open: Mar. – Oct. Mon. – Fri. 9 a.m. – 6 p.m., Sat. 9 a.m. – 4 p.m. and Sun. 10 a.m. – 4 p.m., Nov. – Feb. Mon. – Fri. 9 a.m. – 6.30 p.m. and Sat. 9 a.m. – 1 p.m.

11 17
The numbers 11 – 17 refer to positions marked on the map on pages 2 – 3

CHRONOLOGICAL TABLE

975 First mention in documents.

1254 Town charter granted.

1373 The Wettin family become the feudal lords of the Weimar area.

1525 The Reformation comes to the area.

1547 Weimar becomes the royal capital of the Duchy of Saxe-Weimar.

1552 Lucas Cranach the Elder of Wittenberg comes to Weimar as part of the royal entourage of John Frederick the Magnanimous.

1708 Bach is a violinist and court organist and later leader of the court orchestra.

1775 Carl August ascends to the throne and Goethe comes to Weimar.

1799 Schiller moves from Jena to Weimar.

1815 The Vienna Congress elevates Saxe-Weimar-Eisenach to grand duchy.

1816 Carl August is one of the first German princes to give his land a constitution.

1842 Franz Liszt has the honorary title of Kapellmeister Extraordinary bestowed upon him and in 1848 is permanently called to Weimar.

The Bach memorial on the south side of the Rotes Schloss, opposite the Franz Liszt conservatoire (left). Statue of Wieland (right) on the square named after him on the edge of the city centre.

1759 Duchess Anna Amalia rules in place of her son Carl August, still a minor.

1772 The poet and author Christoph Martin Wieland is made tutor to the heir to the throne Carl August.

1860 The Großherzogliche Kunstschule is founded (the art school is made an art college in 1910).

1872 The Weimarer Orchesterschule is founded (and is a music conservatoire from 1930 onwards).

1885 The Goethe National Museum, Goethe Archives and Goethe Society are founded.

1897 Friedrich Nietzsche, mentally ill, comes to Weimar in the care of his sister Elisabeth.

1902 Henry van de Velde launches an arts and crafts seminar which in 1908 becomes a school of arts and crafts (the Kunstgewerbeschule).

1919 At the theatre, the National Assembly announces the birth of the Weimar Republic. The Staatliches Bauhaus is founded under Walter Gropius.

1920 Weimar is made the capital of the Free State of Thuringia.

1937 The Nazis build Buchenwald Concentration Camp.

1945 Air raids destroy parts of the old town, the theatre, and museums.

1949 The Goethehaus is reopened. Thomas Mann gives a speech in honour of the 200th anniversary of Goethe's birth.

1990 The new government of the Free State of Thuringia is constituted at the Deutsches Nationaltheater.

1993 Weimar applies for and is granted the title of City of Culture 1999.

Friedrich Ebert at the opening speech of the Constituent German National Assembly in the city theatre in Weimar on 6 February 1919.

Airy perspective:
Grand Duke Carl August
on horseback.

INDEX

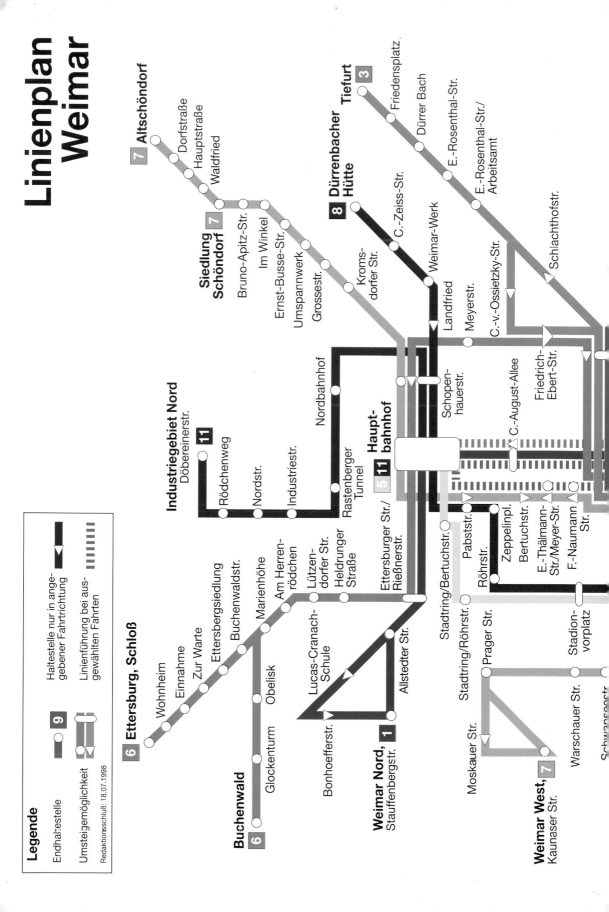

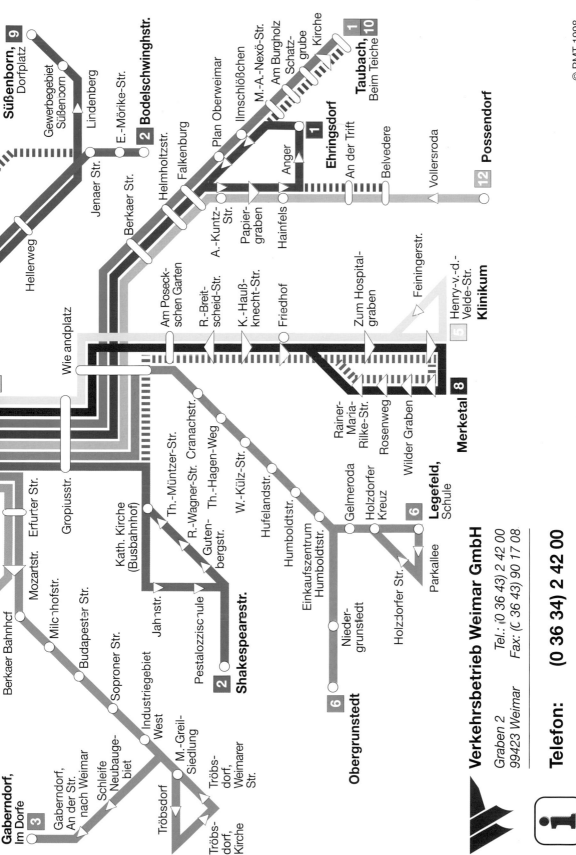

Süßenborn, **9**
Dorfplatz

Gewerbegebiet Süßenborn

Lindenberg

E.-Mörike-Str.

Jenaer Str.

Berkaer Str.

Hellerweg

2 Bodelschwinghstr.

Helmholtzstr.

Falkenburg

Plan Oberweimar

Ilmschlößchen

M.-A.-Nexö-Str.

Am Burgholz

Schatz-grube

Kirche

1

Taubach, 10
Beim Teiche

Wieandplatz

A.-Kuntz-Str.

Papier-graben

Hainfels

Anger

Ehringsdorf 1

An der Trift

Belvedere

Vollersroda

12 Possendorf

Am Poseck-schen Garten

R.-Breit-scheid-Str.

K.-Hauß-knecht-Str.

Friedhof

Zum Hospital-graben

Feiningerstr.

Henry-v.-d.-Velde-Str.
Klinikum 5

Rainer-Maria-Rilke-Str.

Rosenweg

Wilder Graben

Merketal 8

Gropiusstr.

Erfurter Str.

Th.-Müntzer-Str.

R.-Wagner-Str. Cranachstr.

Guten-bergstr. Th.-Hagen-Weg

W.-Külz-Str.

Hufelandstr.

Humboldtstr.

Einkaufszentrum Humboldtstr.

Gelmeroda

Holzdorfer Kreuz

Legefeld, **6**
Schule

Mozartstr.

Milchhofstr.

Budapester Str.

Soproner Str.

Kath. Kirche (Busbahnhof)

Jahnstr.

Pestalozzischule

2 Shakespearestr.

Niedergrunstedt

Holzdorfer Str.

Parkallee

6 Obergrunstedt

Berkaer Bahnhof

Industriegebiet West

Gaberndorf, 3
Im Dorfe

Gaberndorf, An der Str. nach Weimar

Schleife Neubauge-biet

M.-Greil-Siedlung

Tröbsdorf

Tröbsdorf, Weimarer Str.

Tröbsdorf, Kirche

© RMT 1998

▼ **Verkehrsbetrieb Weimar GmbH**

Graben 2   Tel.: (0 36 43) 2 42 00
99423 Weimar   Fax: (0 36 43) 90 17 08

Telefon: (0 36 34) 2 42 00

Stürtz-REGIO –
Practical, packed with
illustrations – great souvenirs.
Stürtz Verlag GmbH,
Beethovenstraße 5
D-97080 Würzburg